MW00380812

DOGS

Coloring Book for Adults

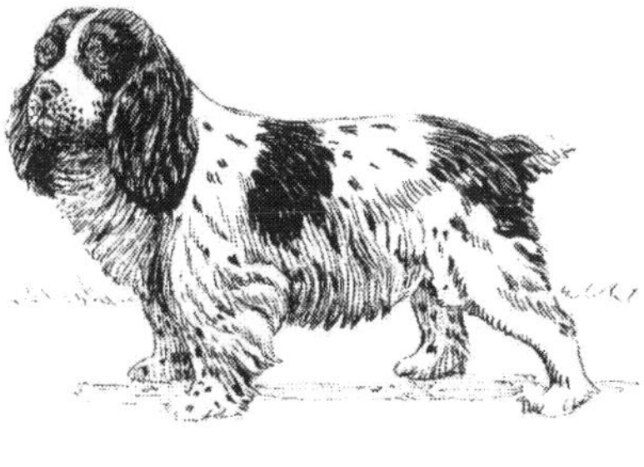

Yap Kee Chong
8345 NW 66 ST #B7885
Miami, FL 33166

Createspace

THIS BOOK BELONGS TO

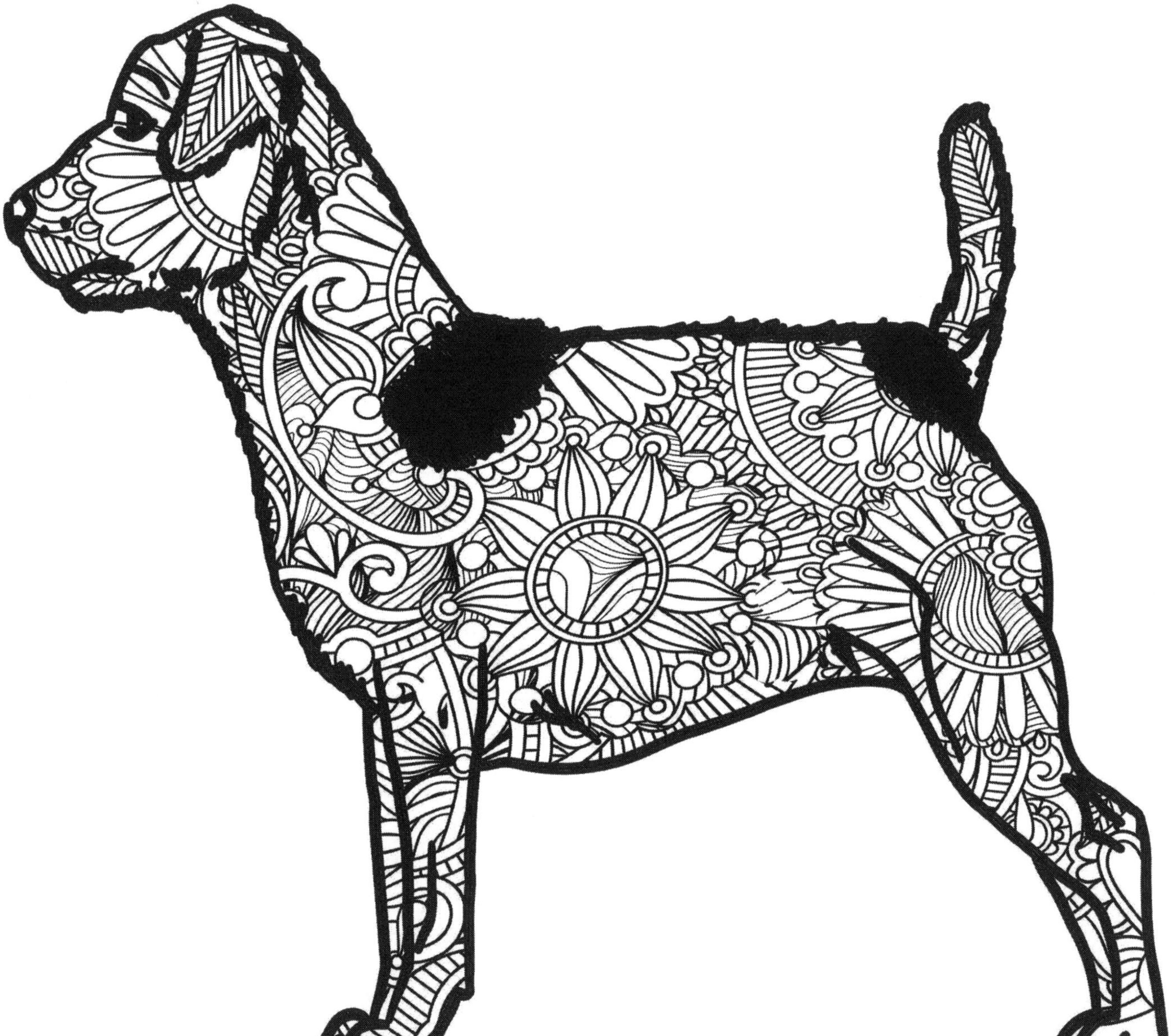

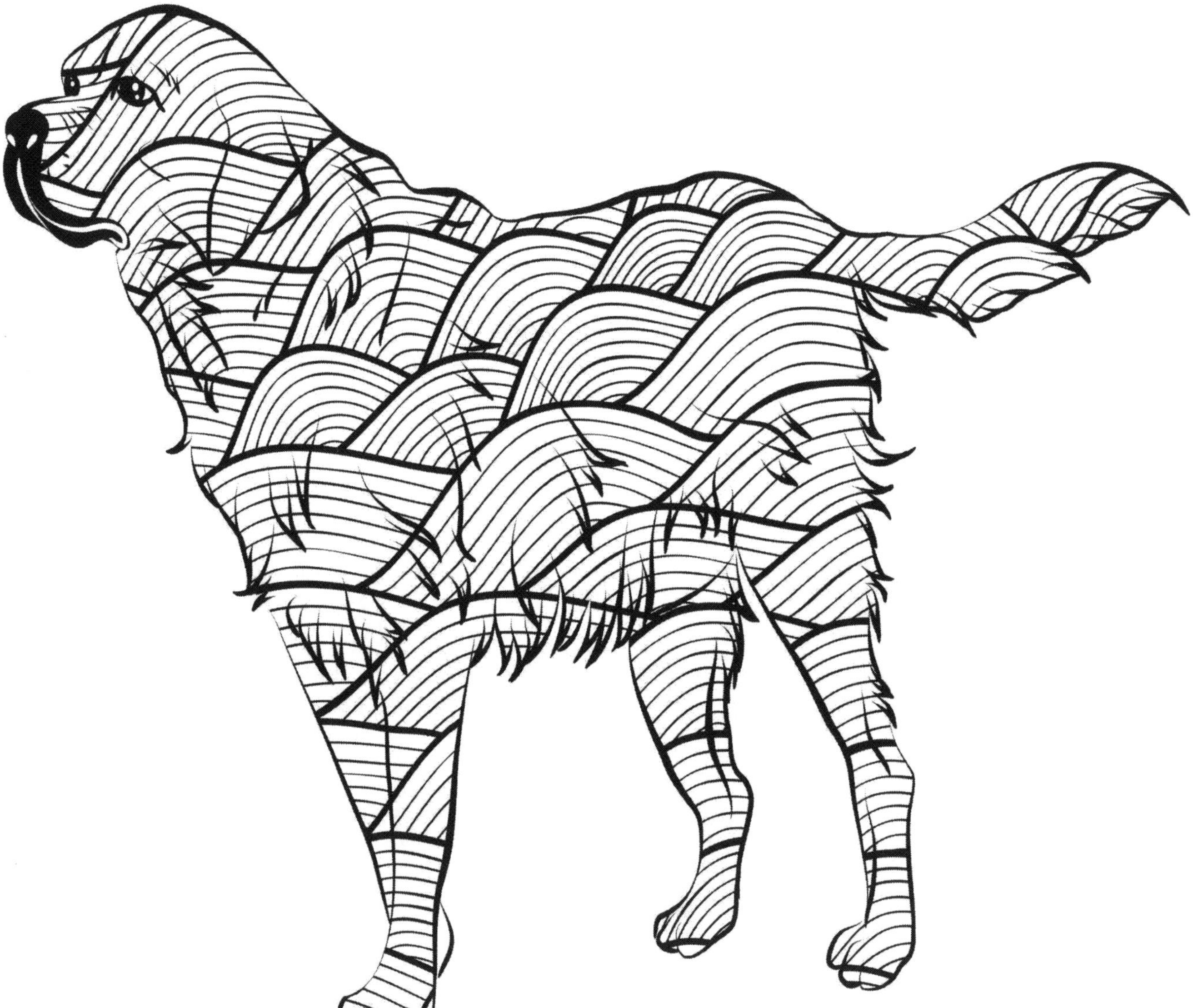

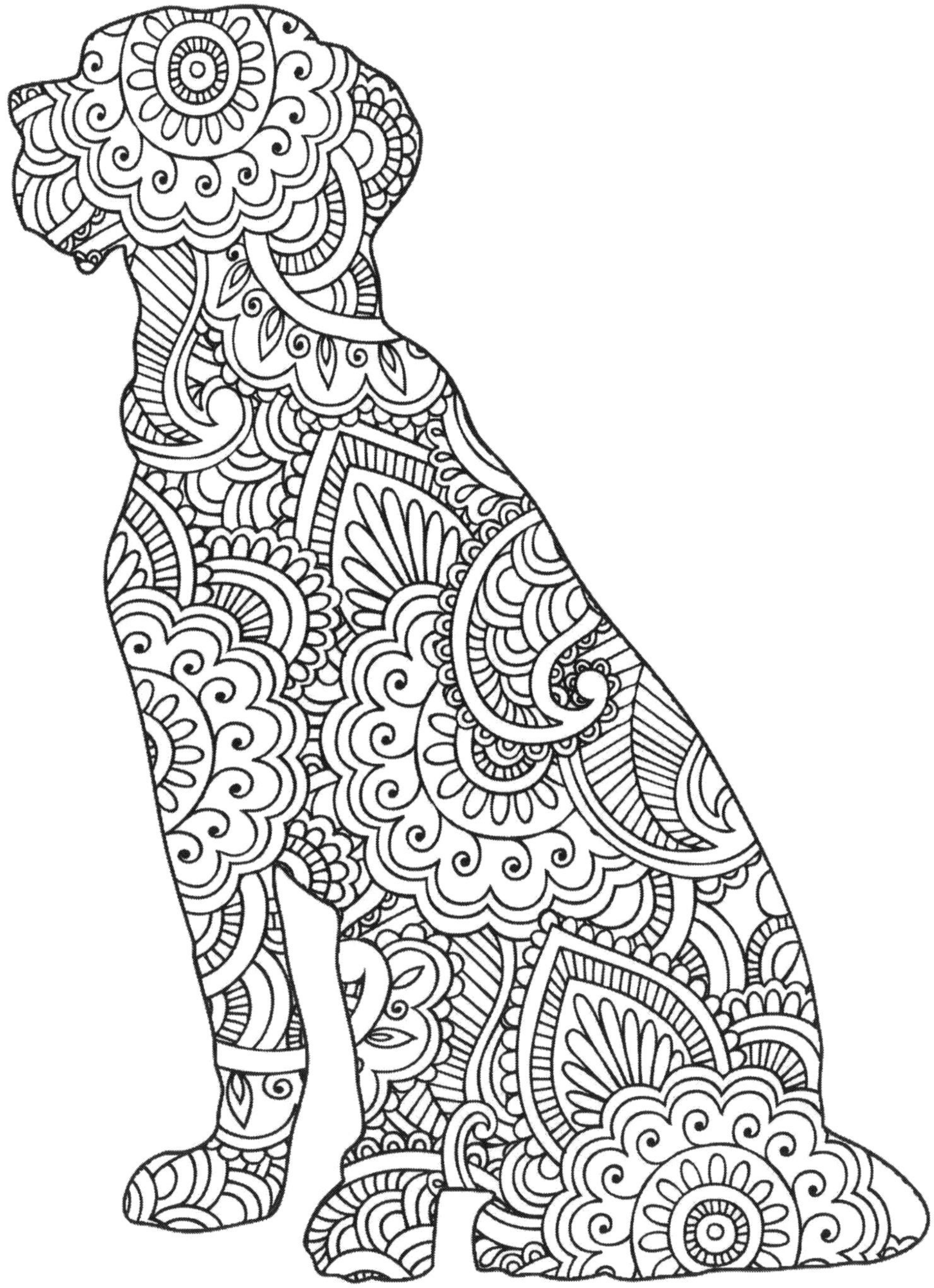

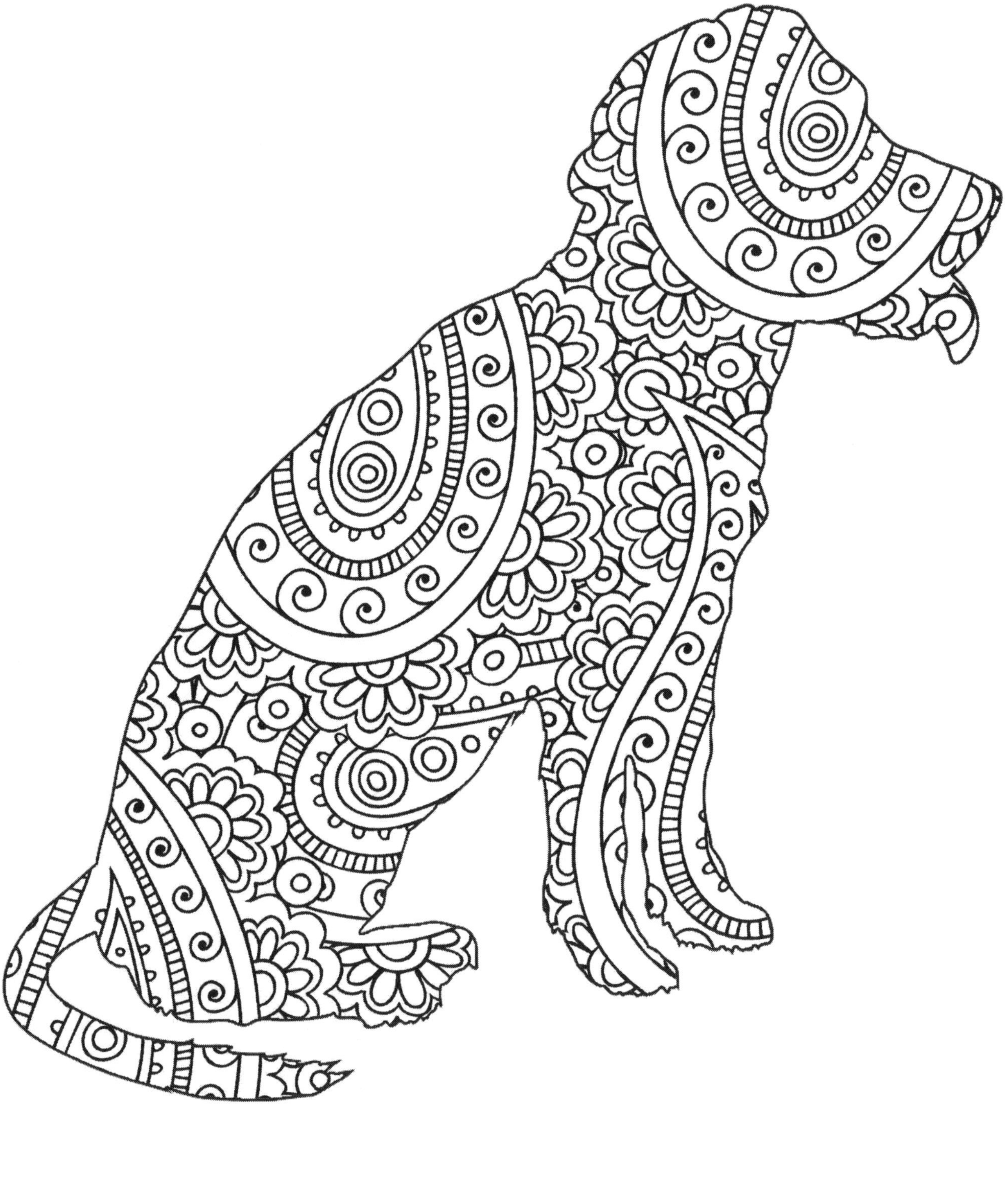

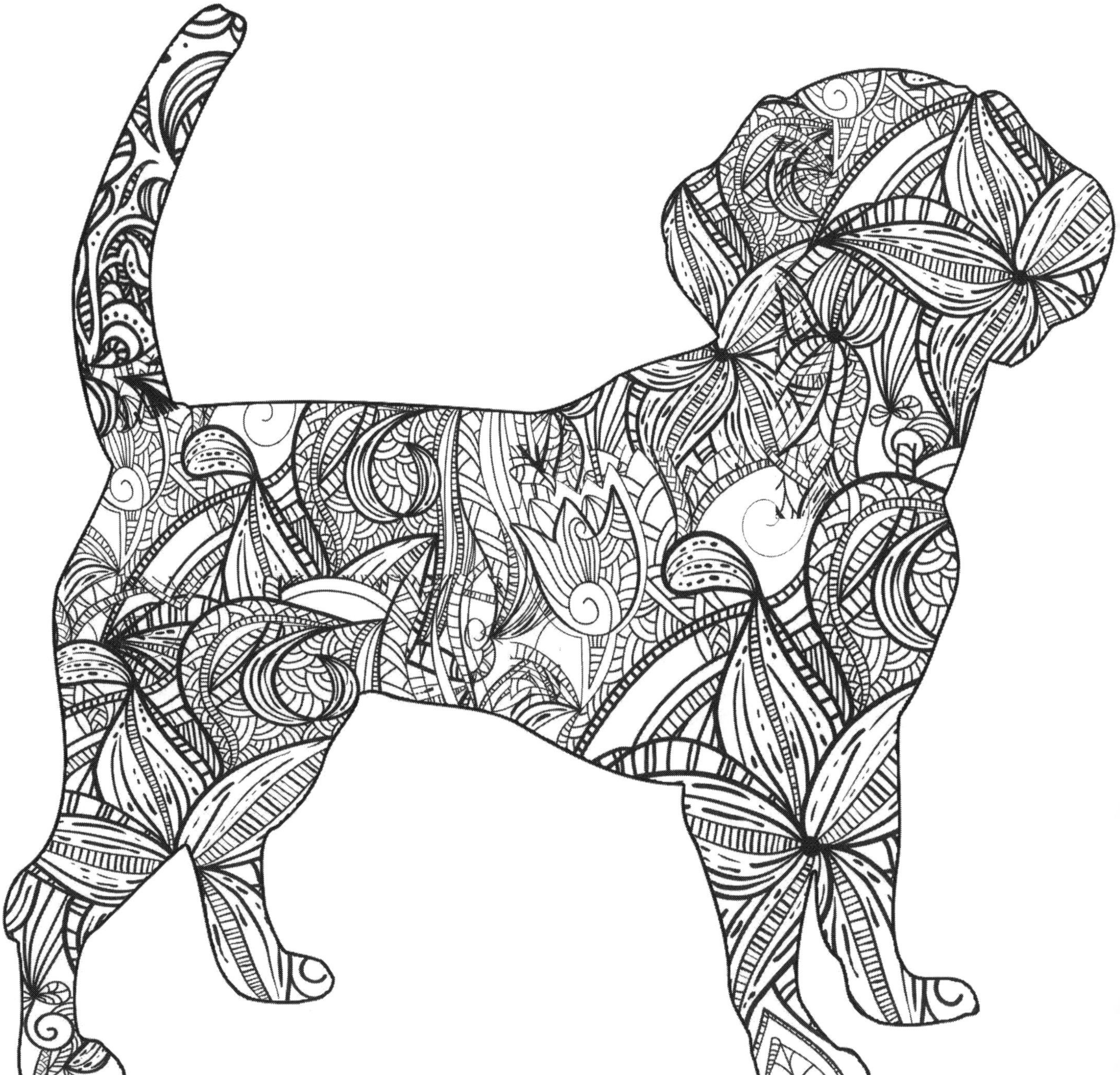

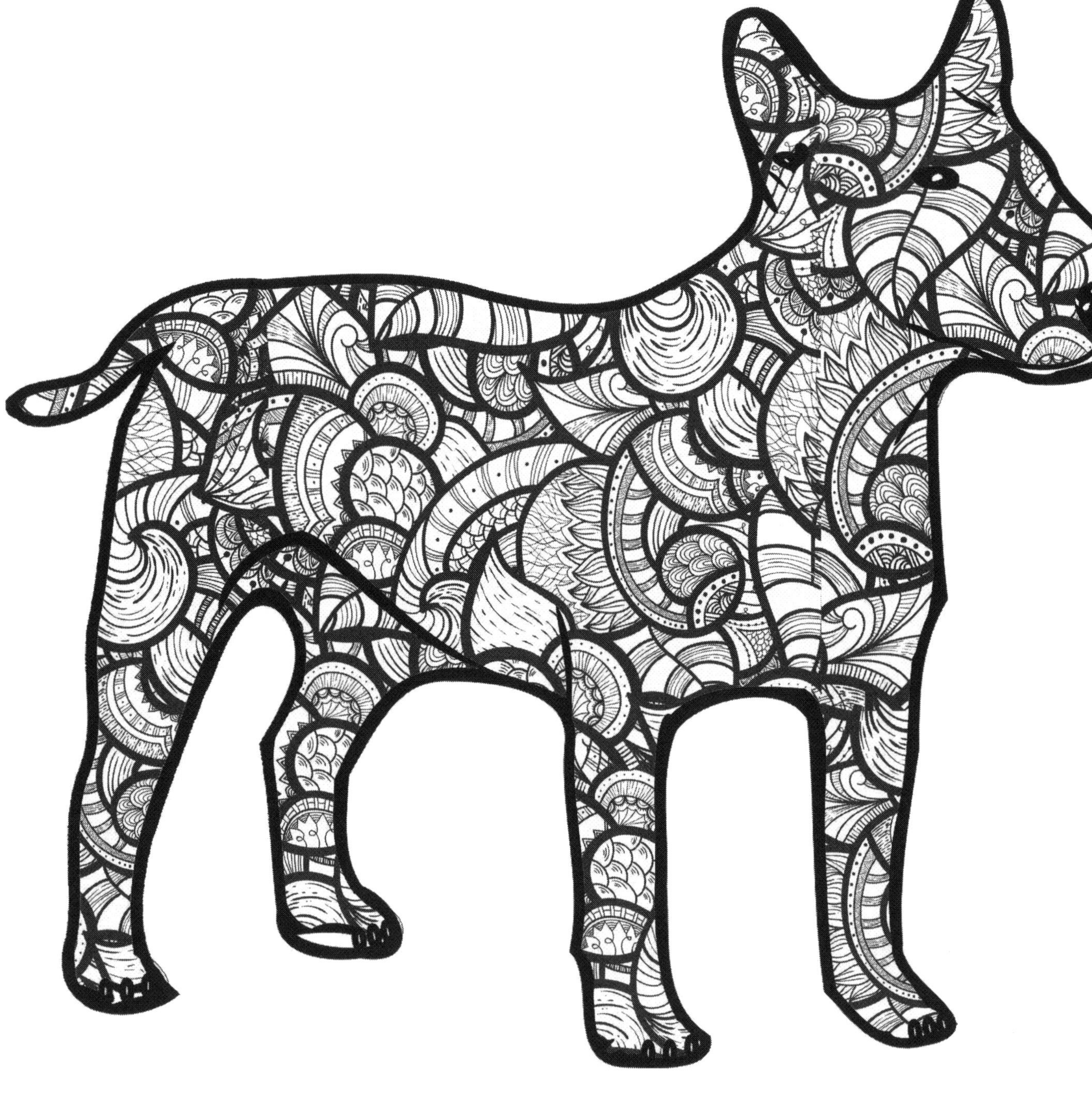

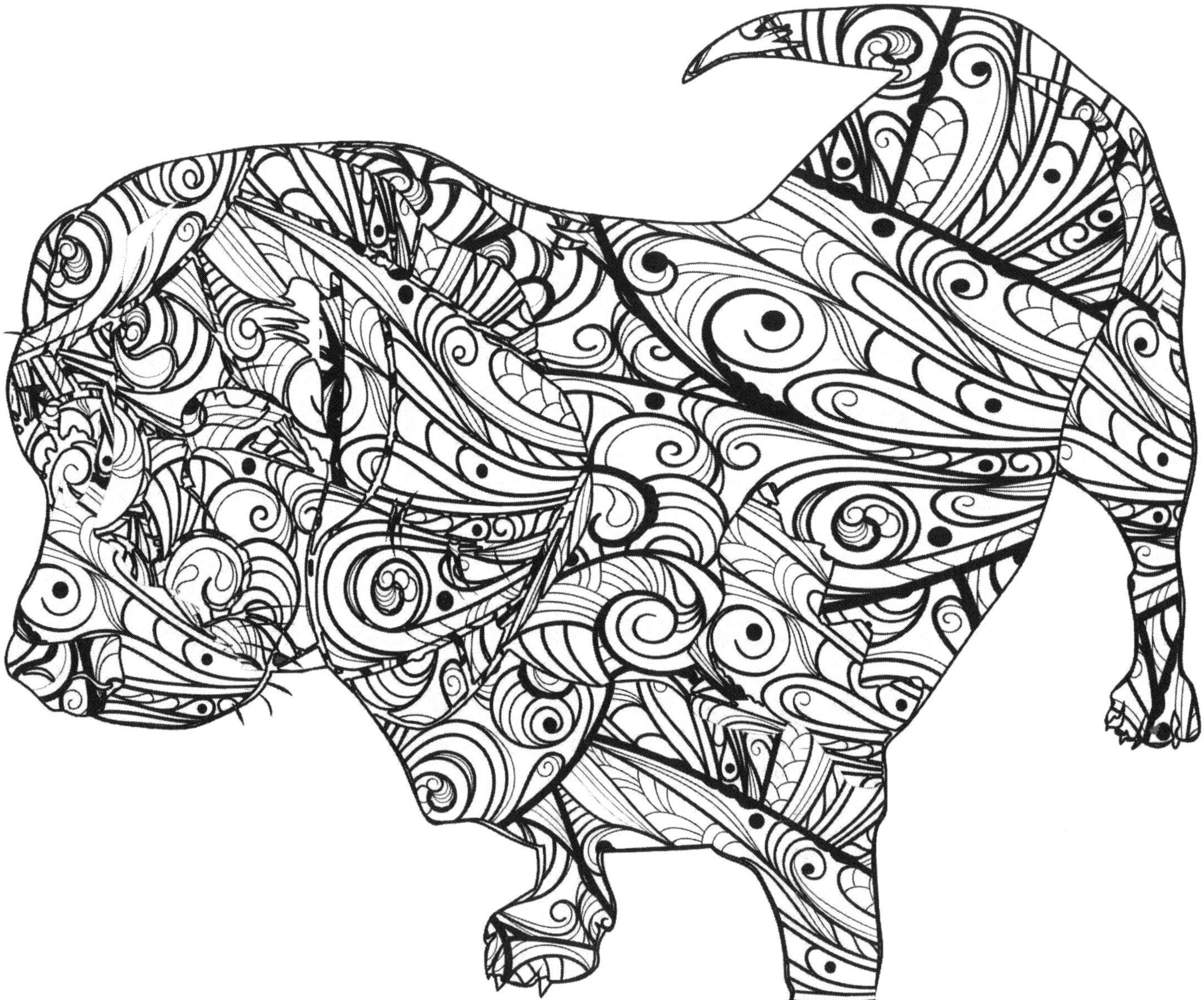

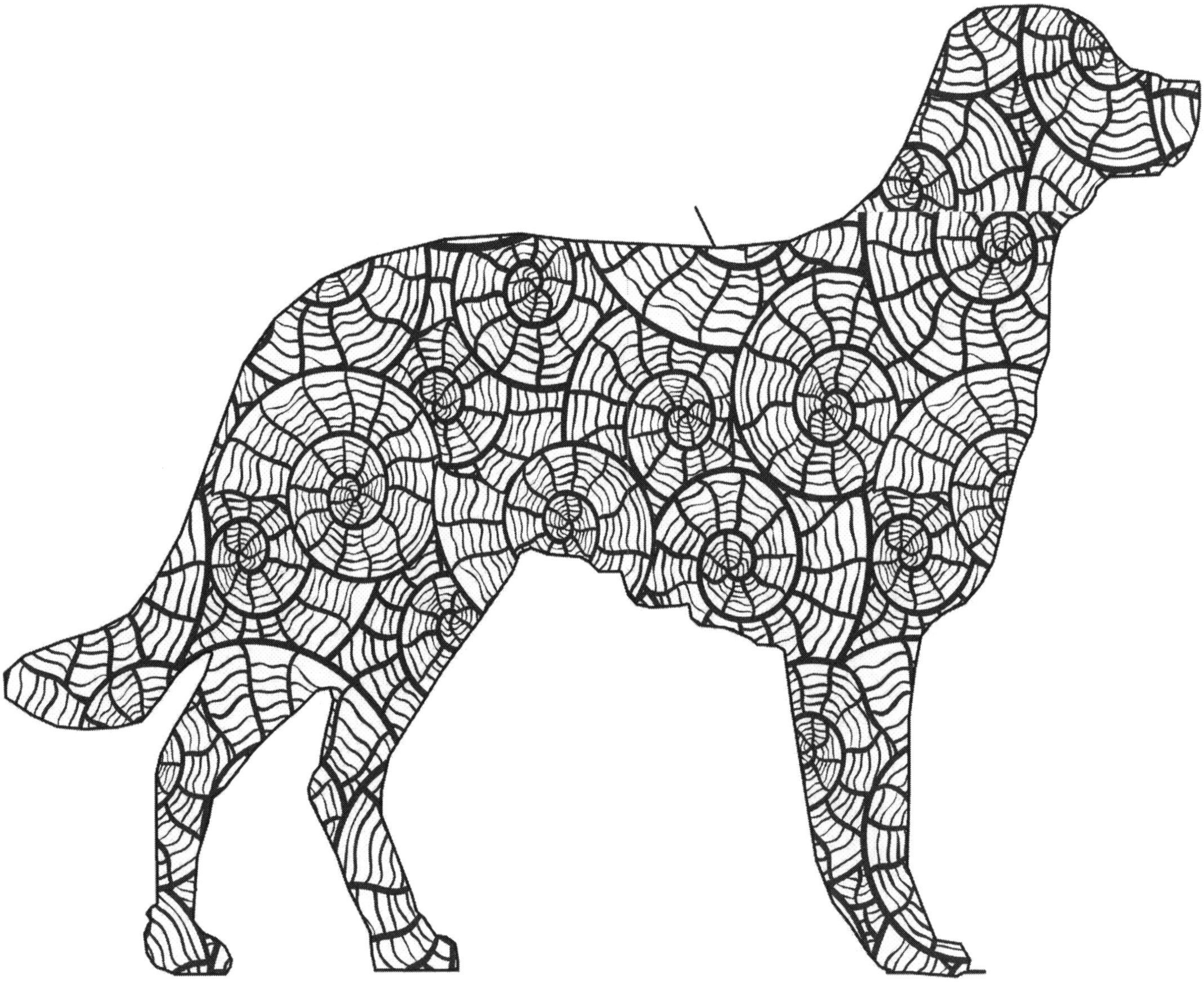

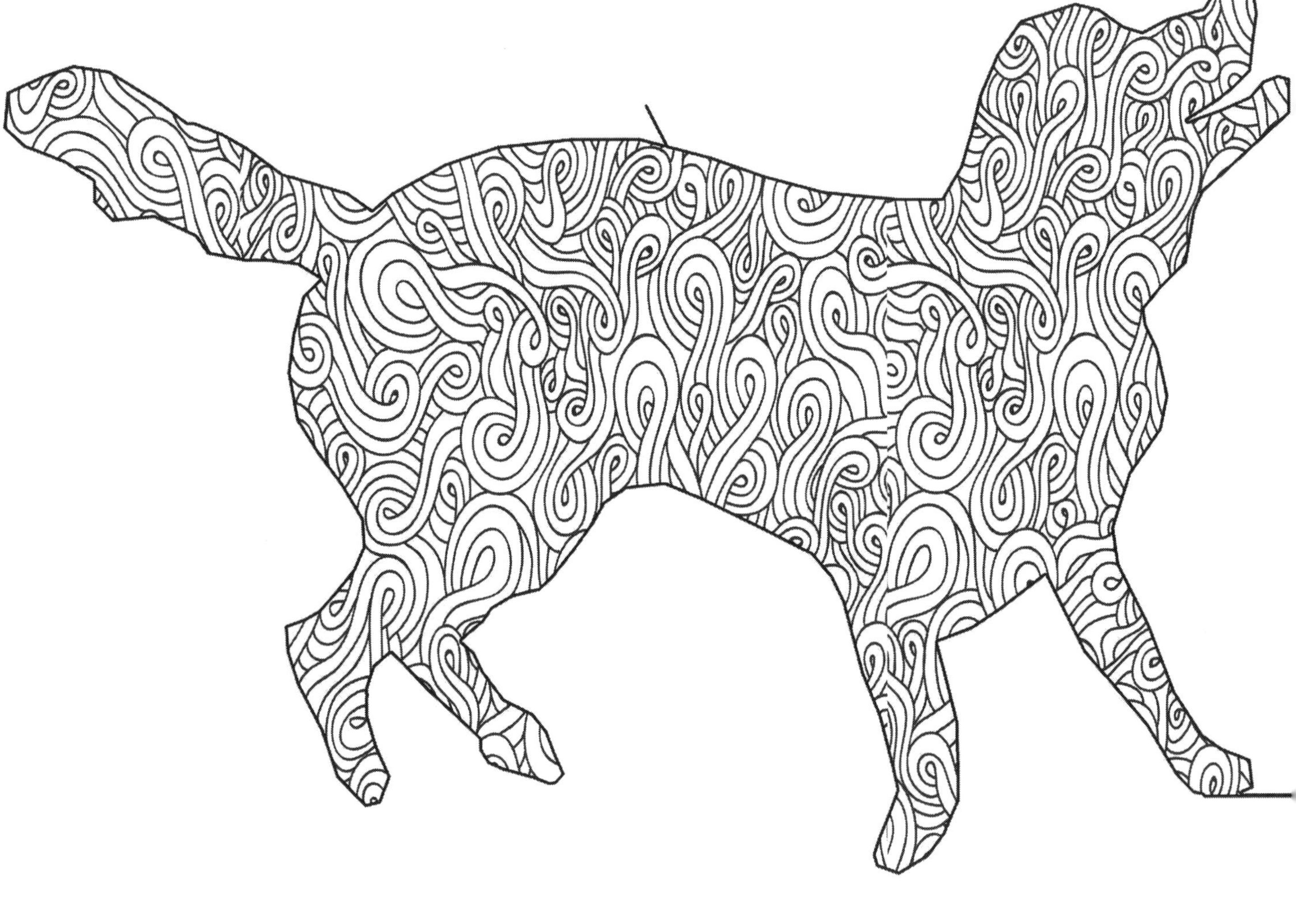

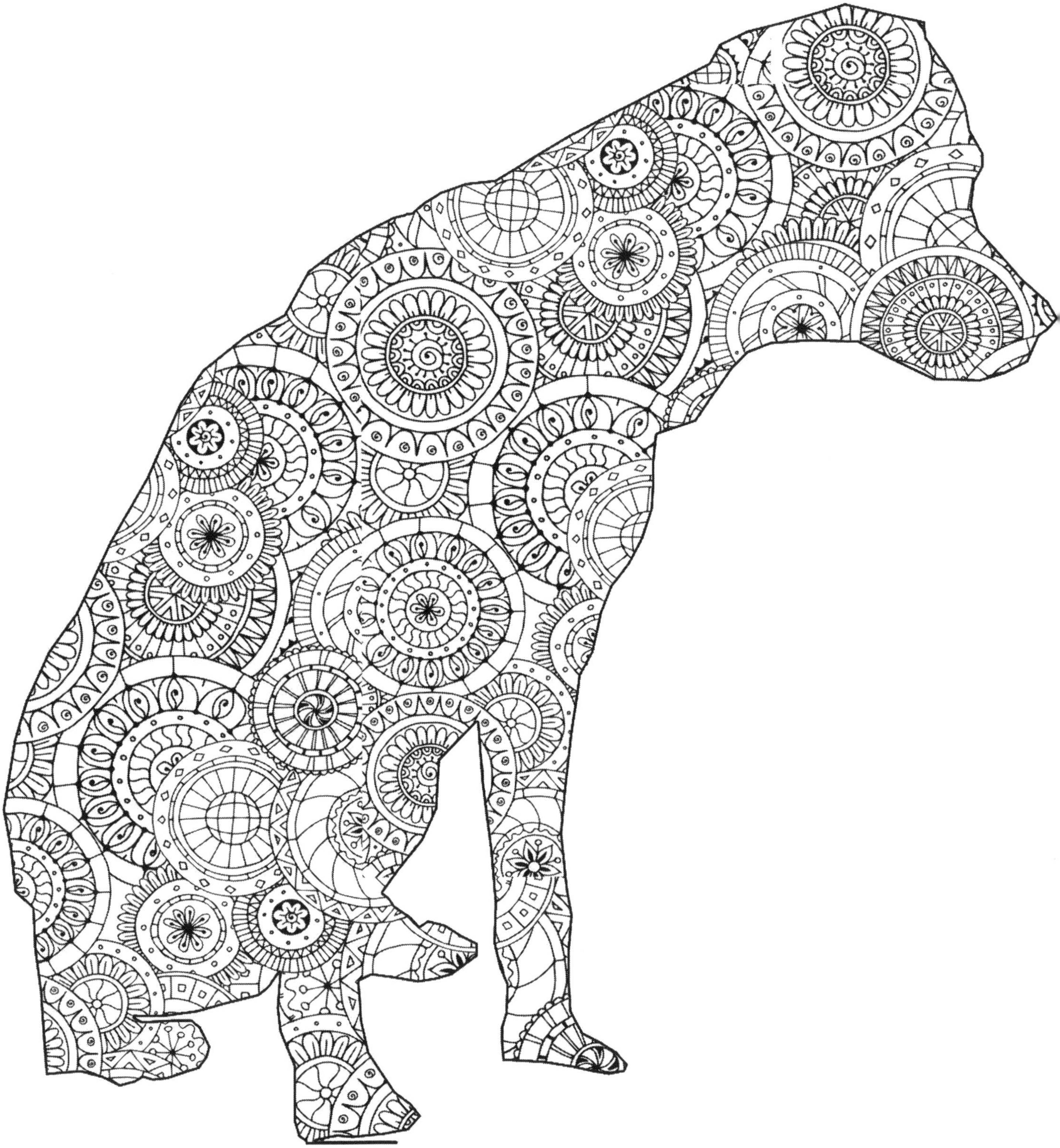

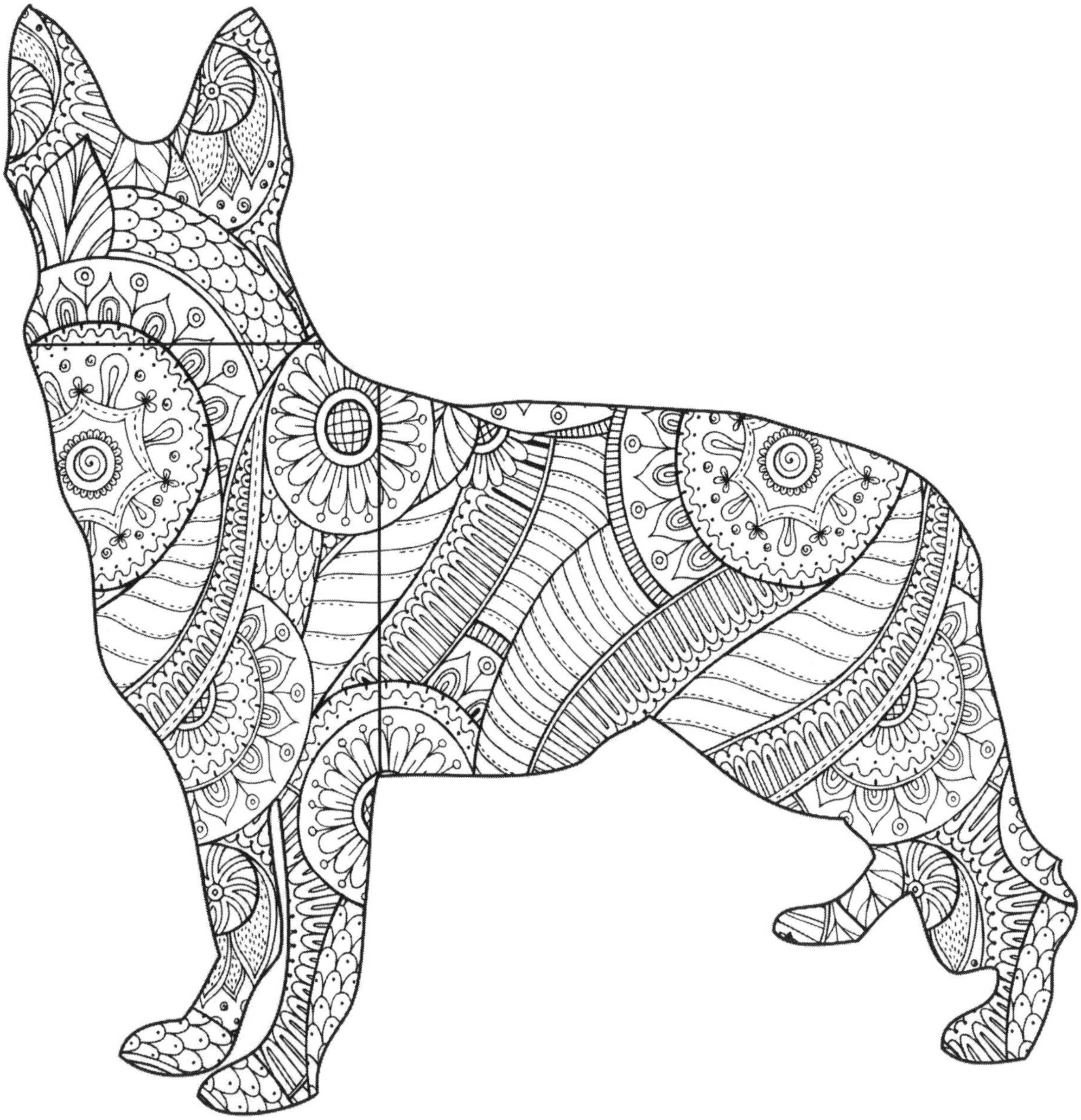

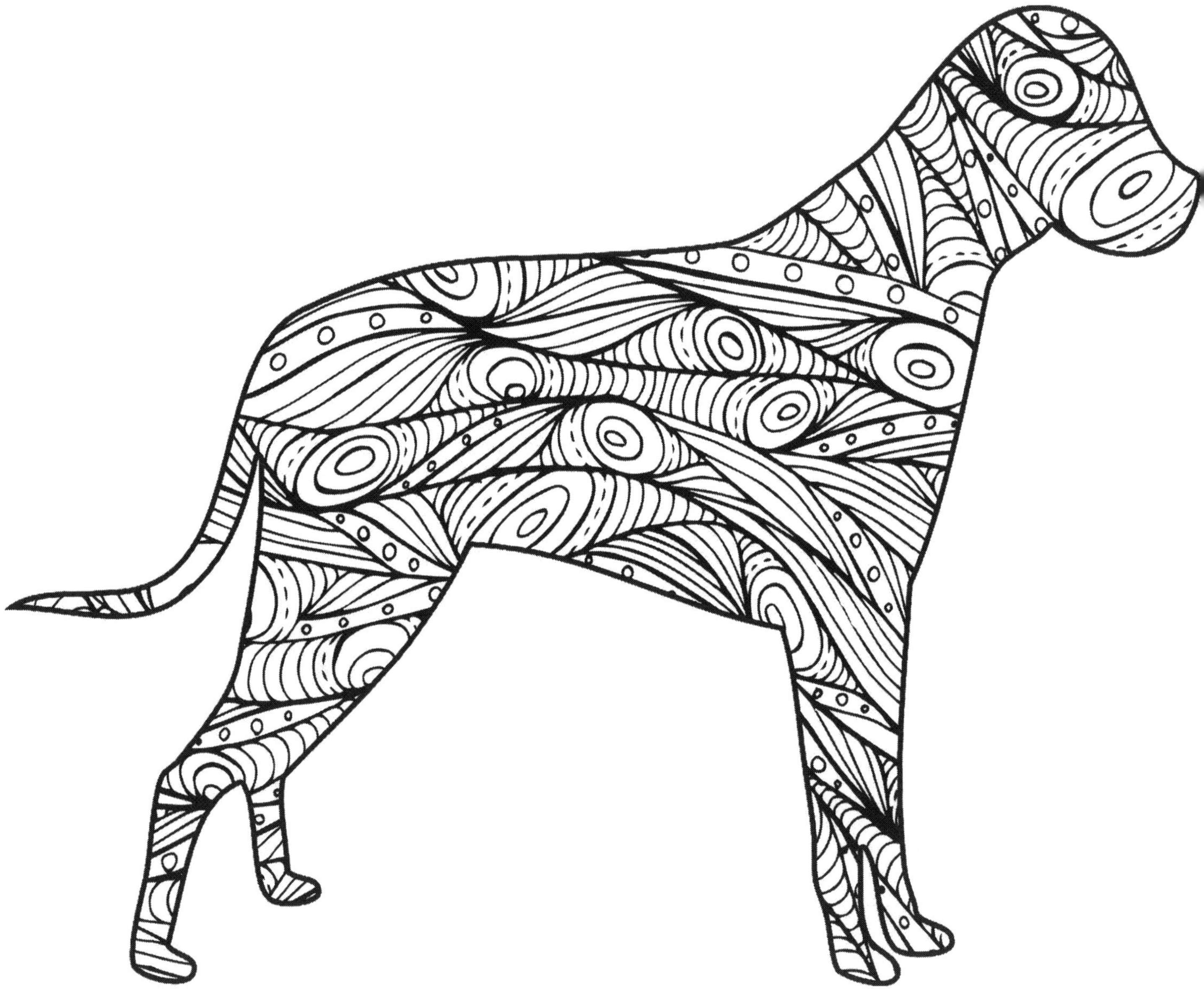

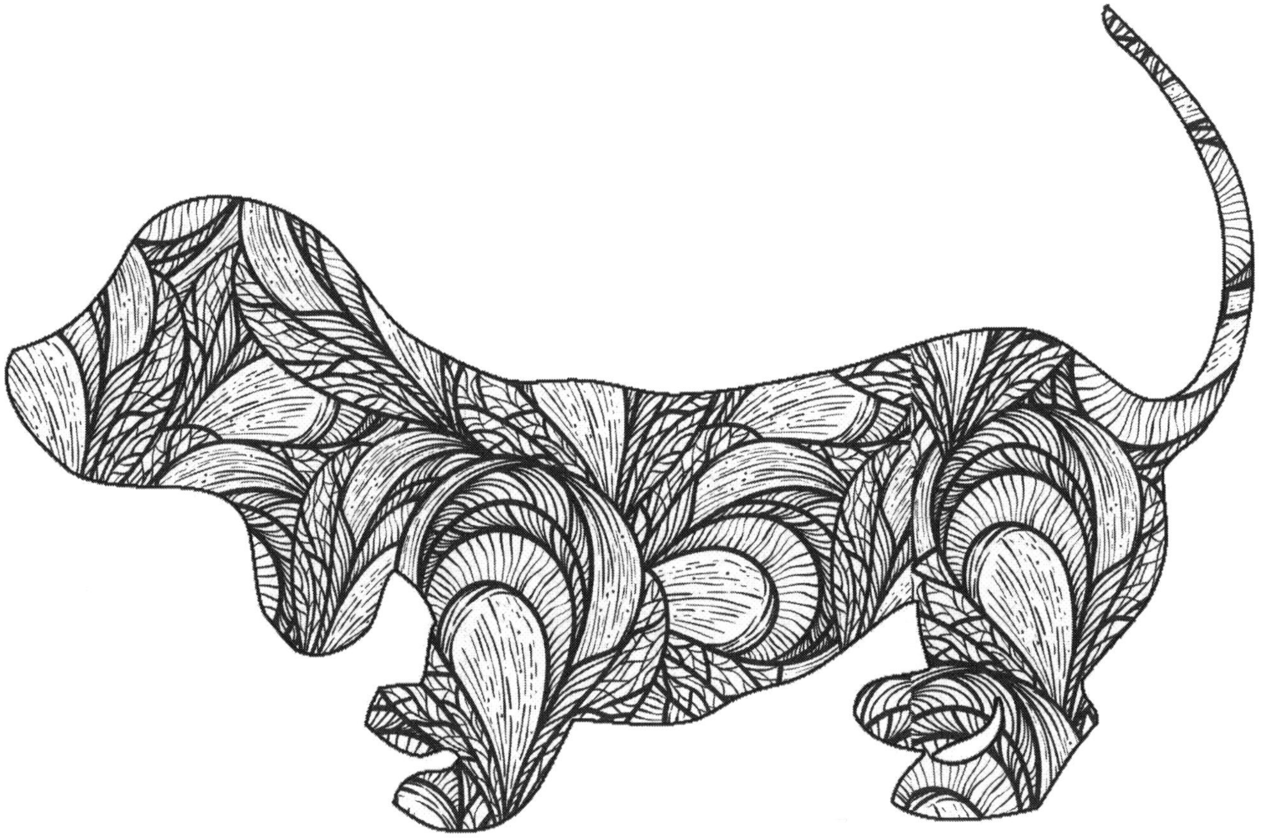

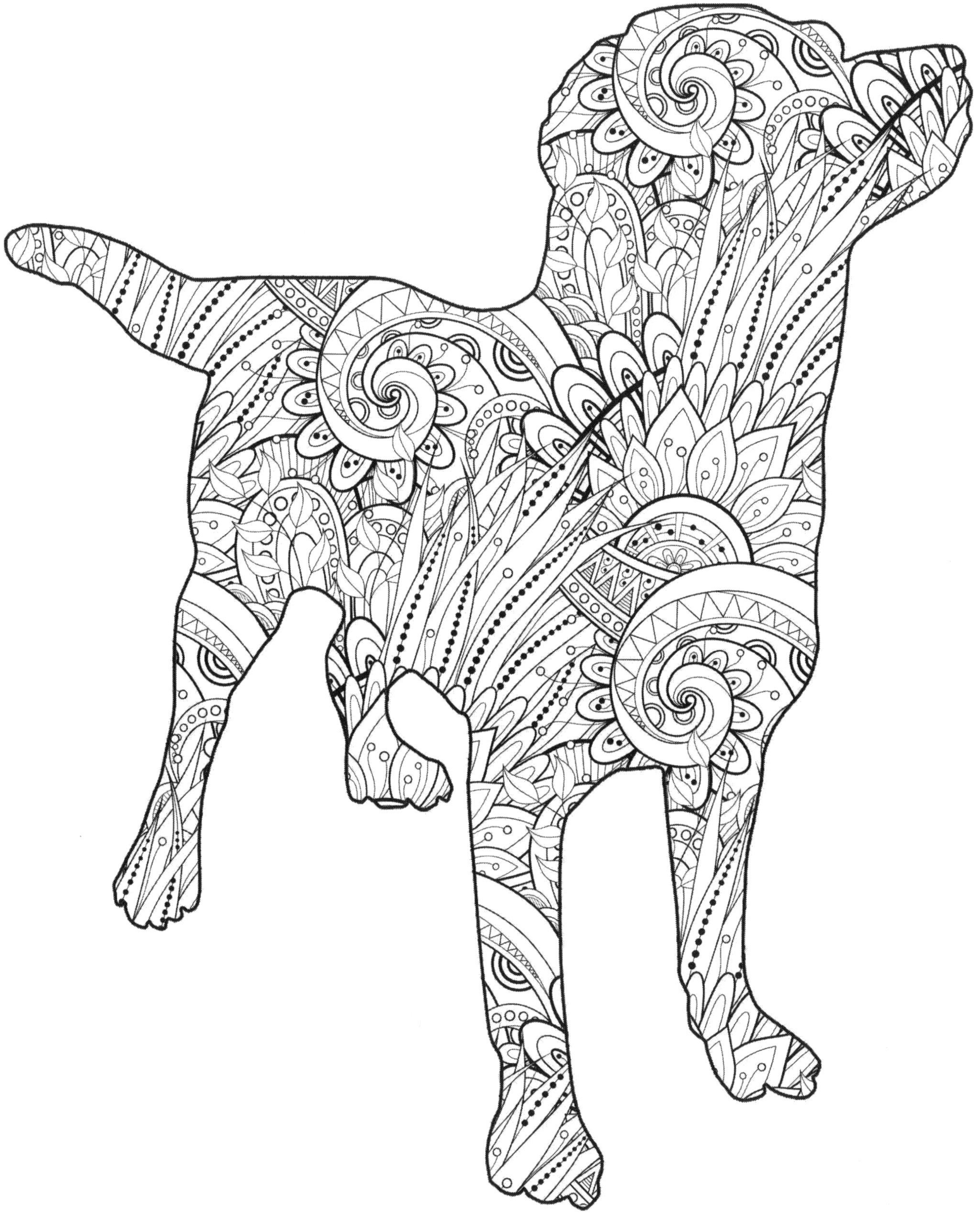

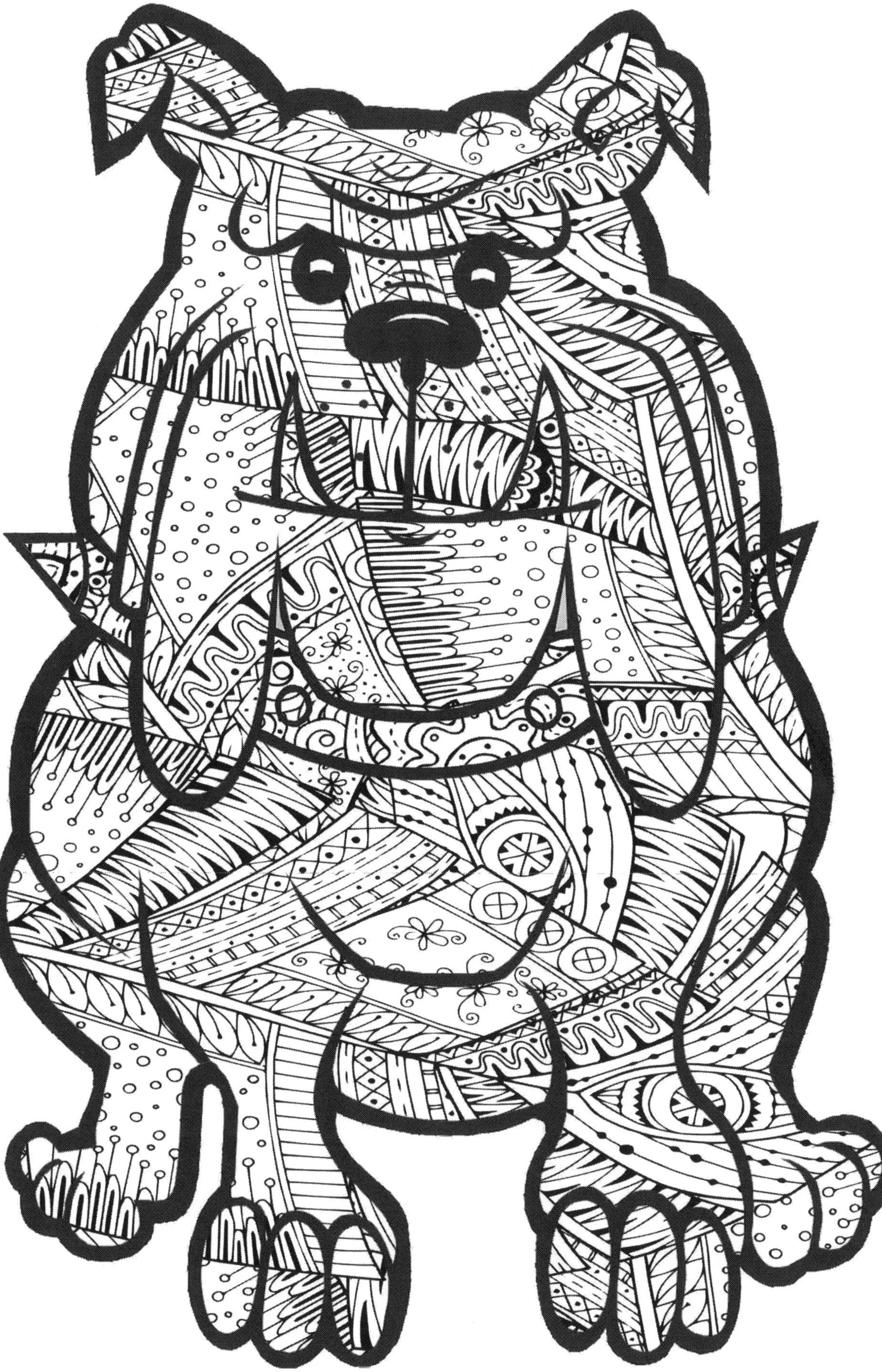

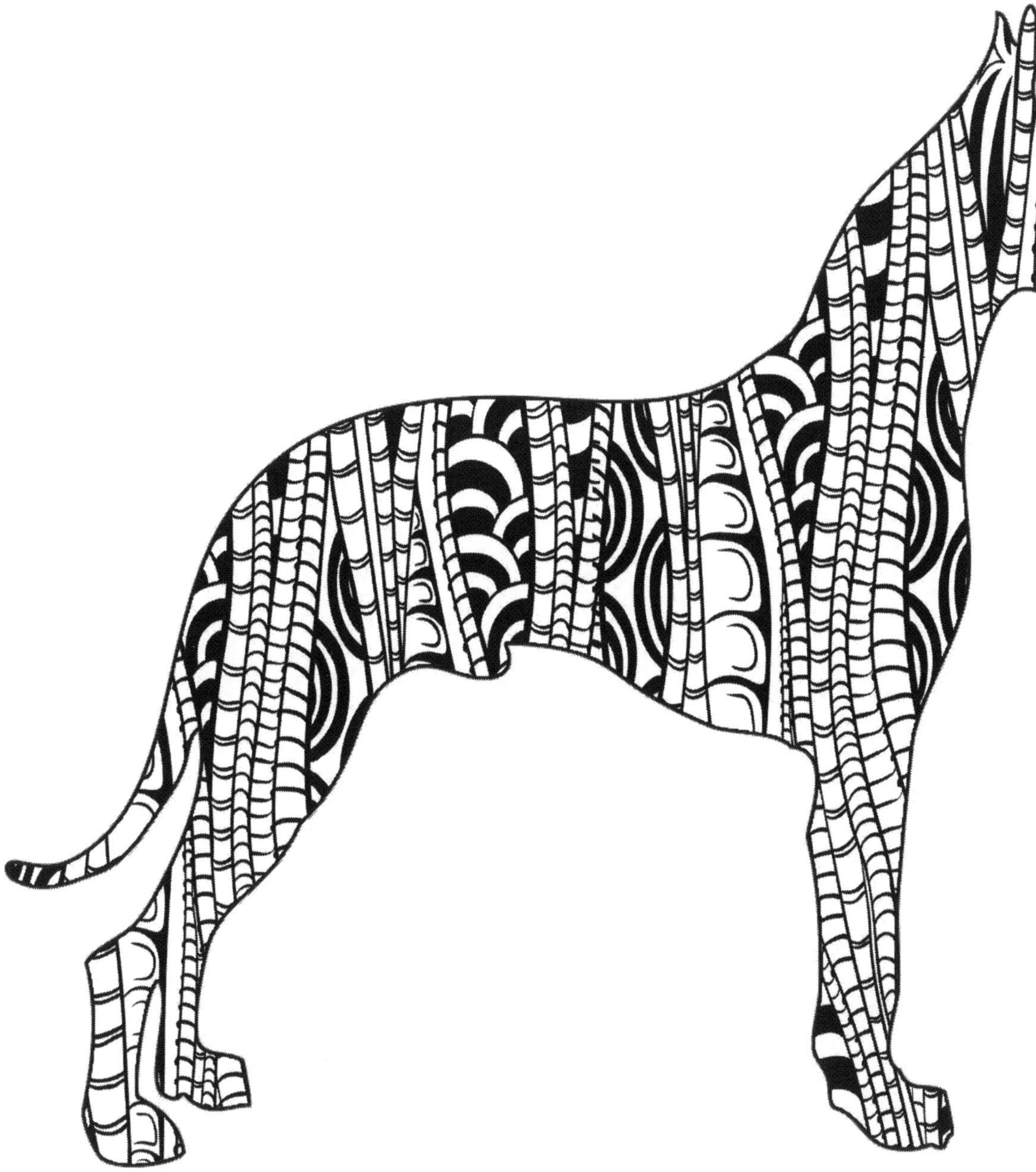

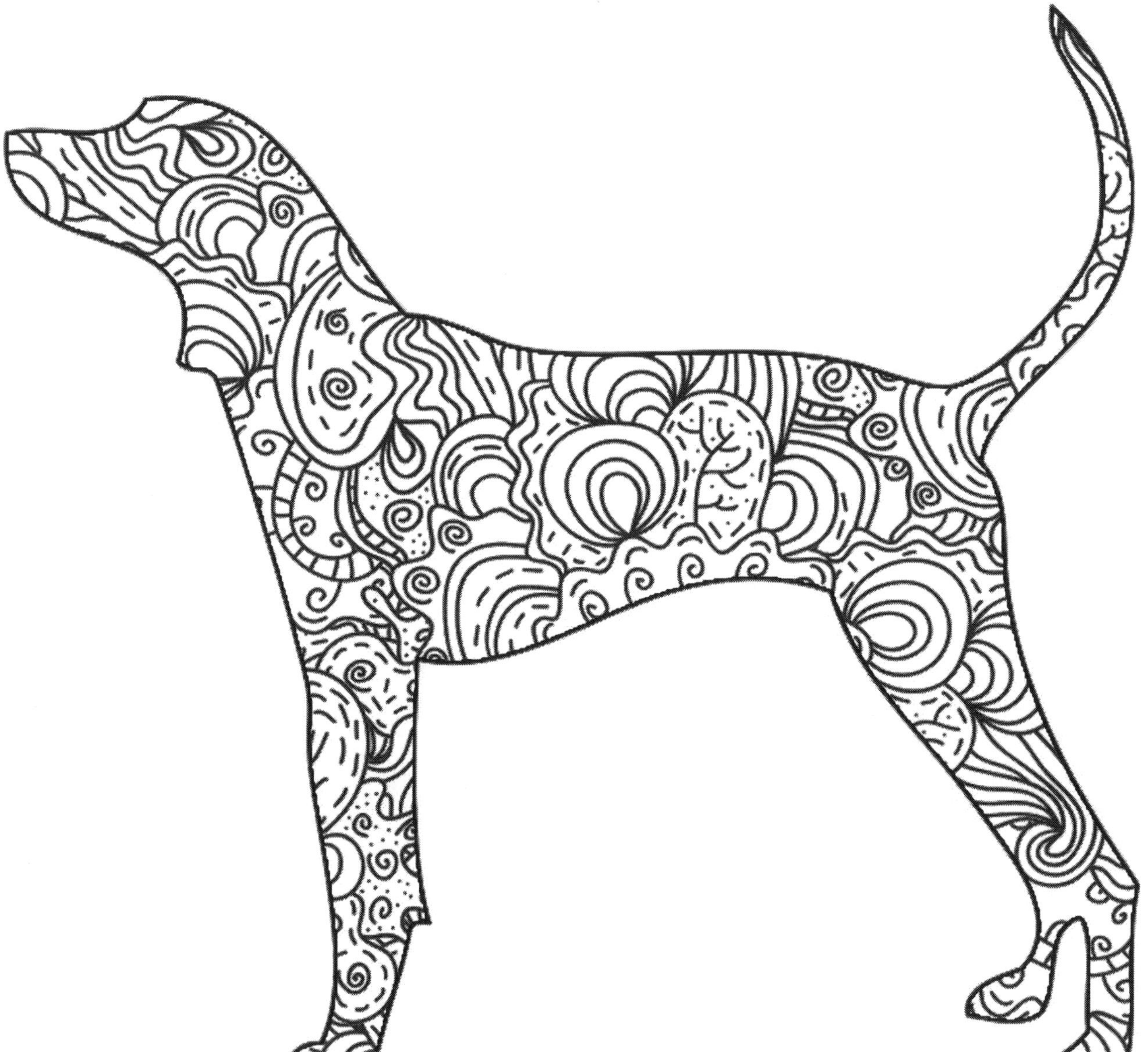

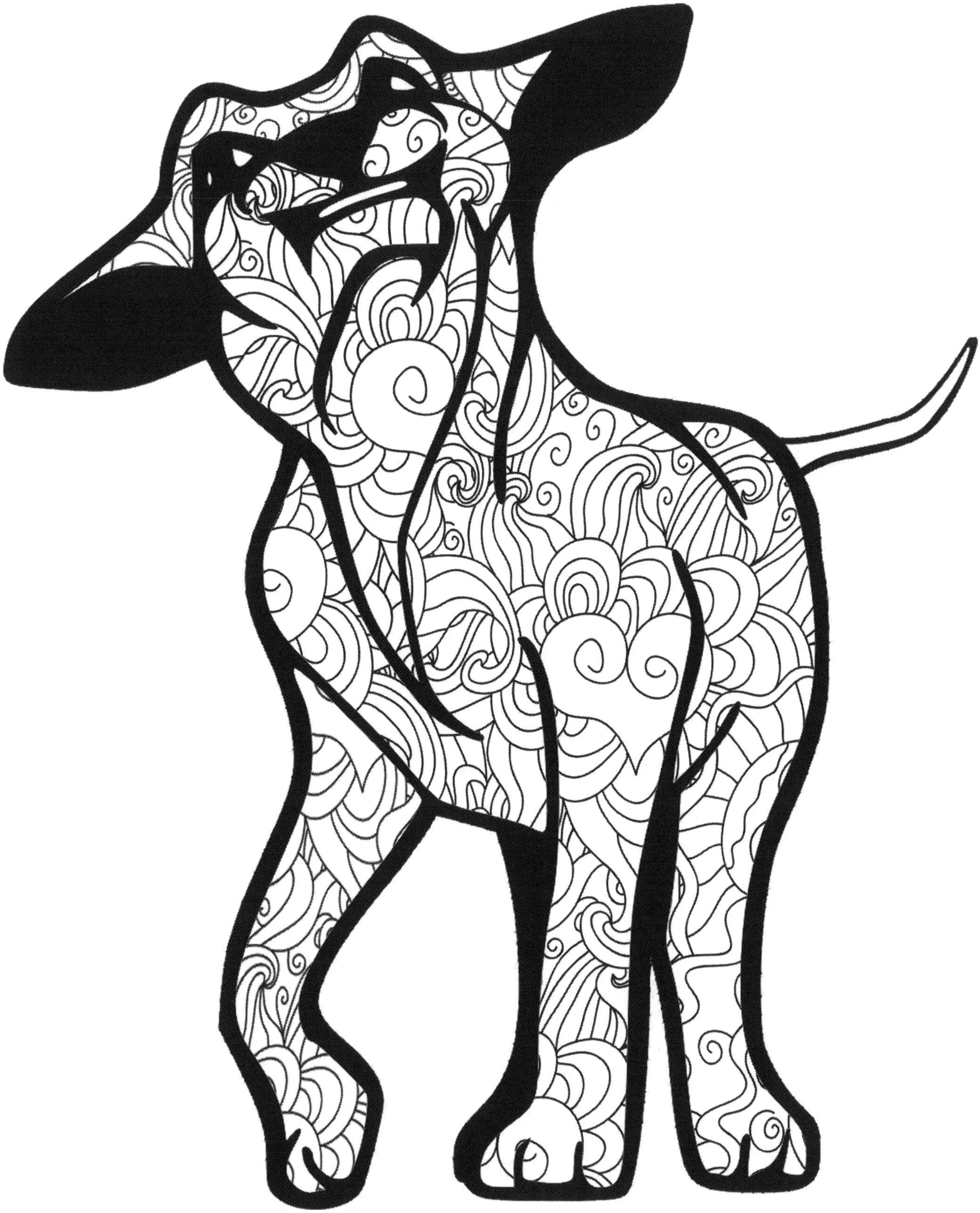

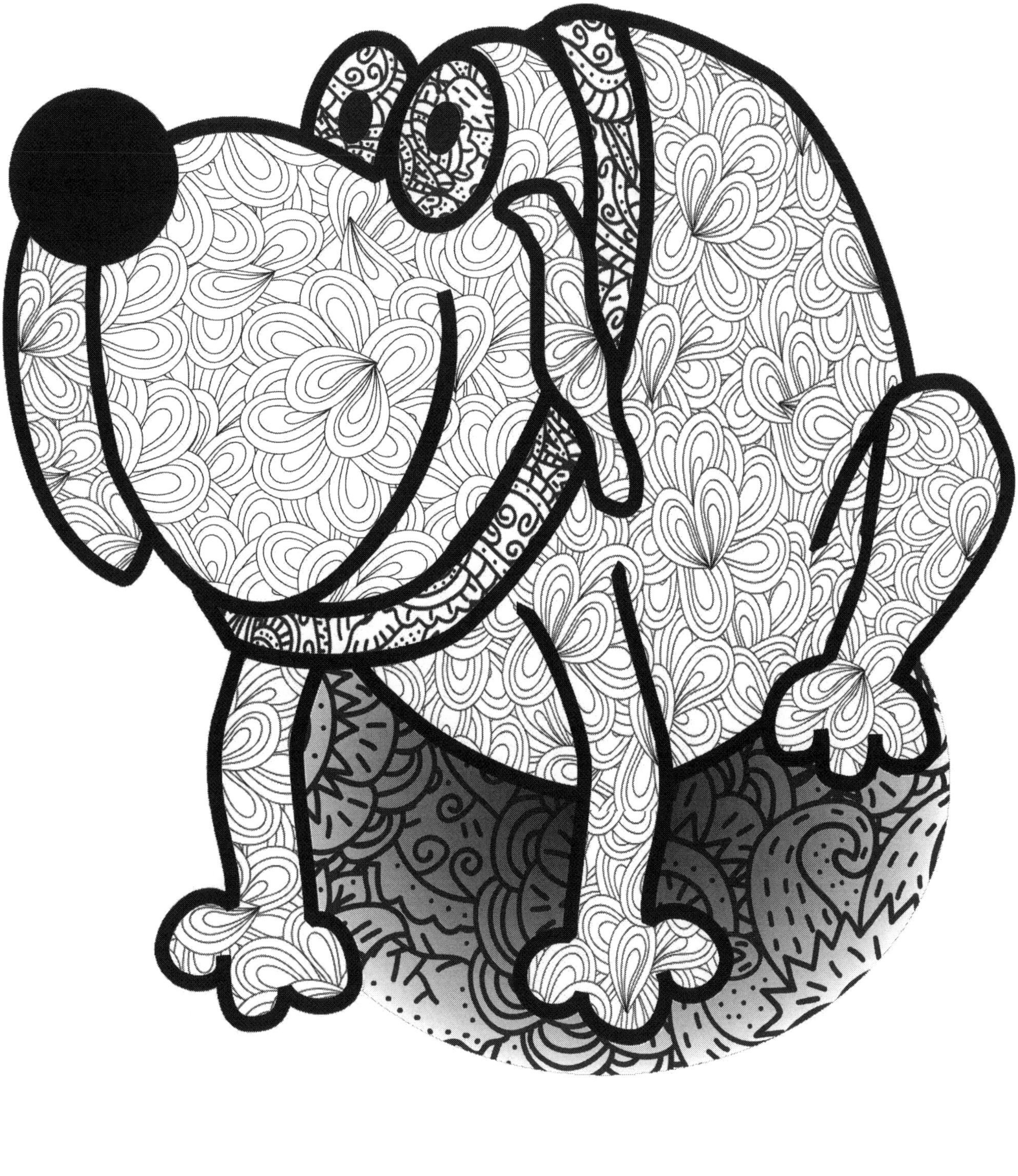

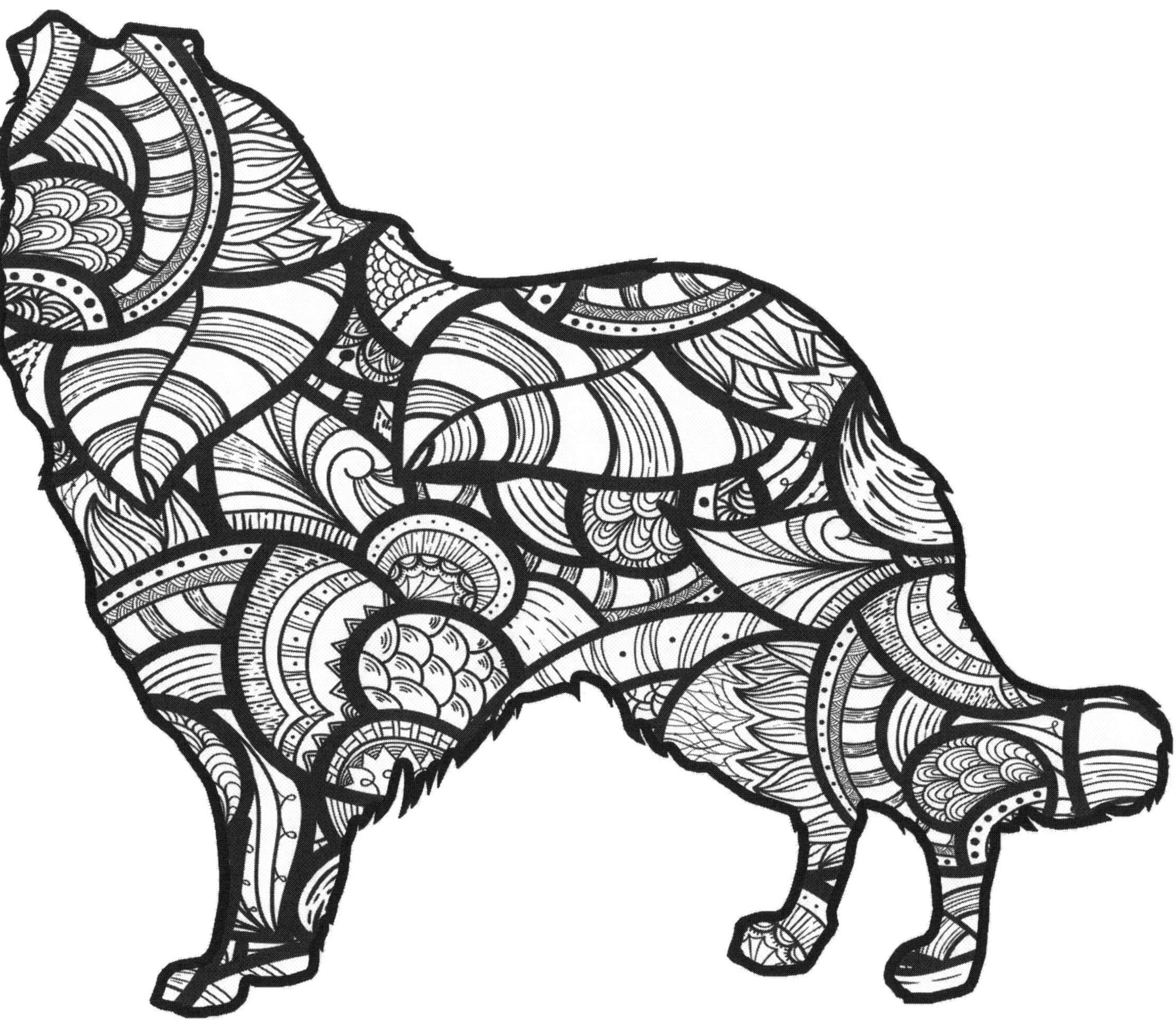

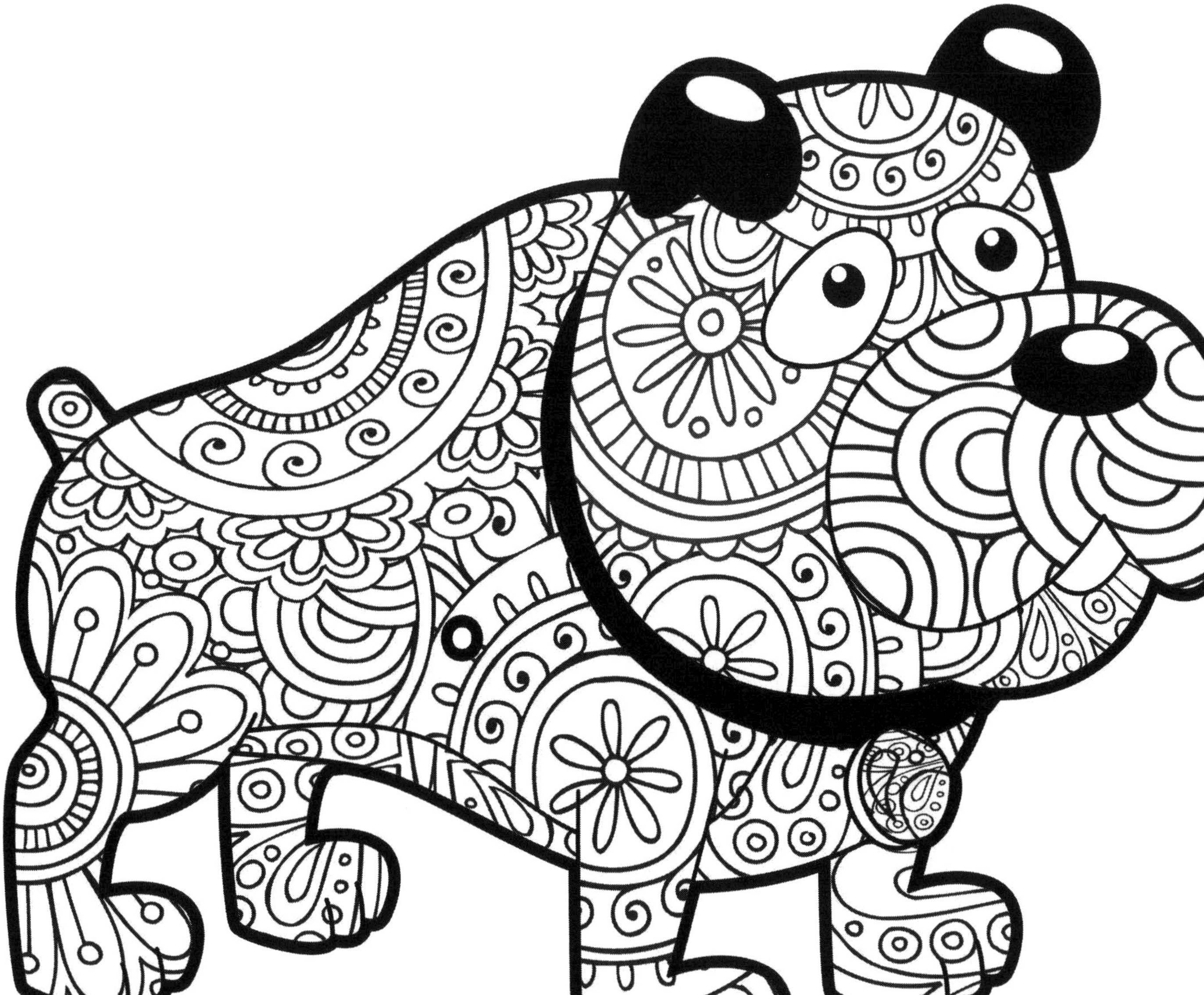

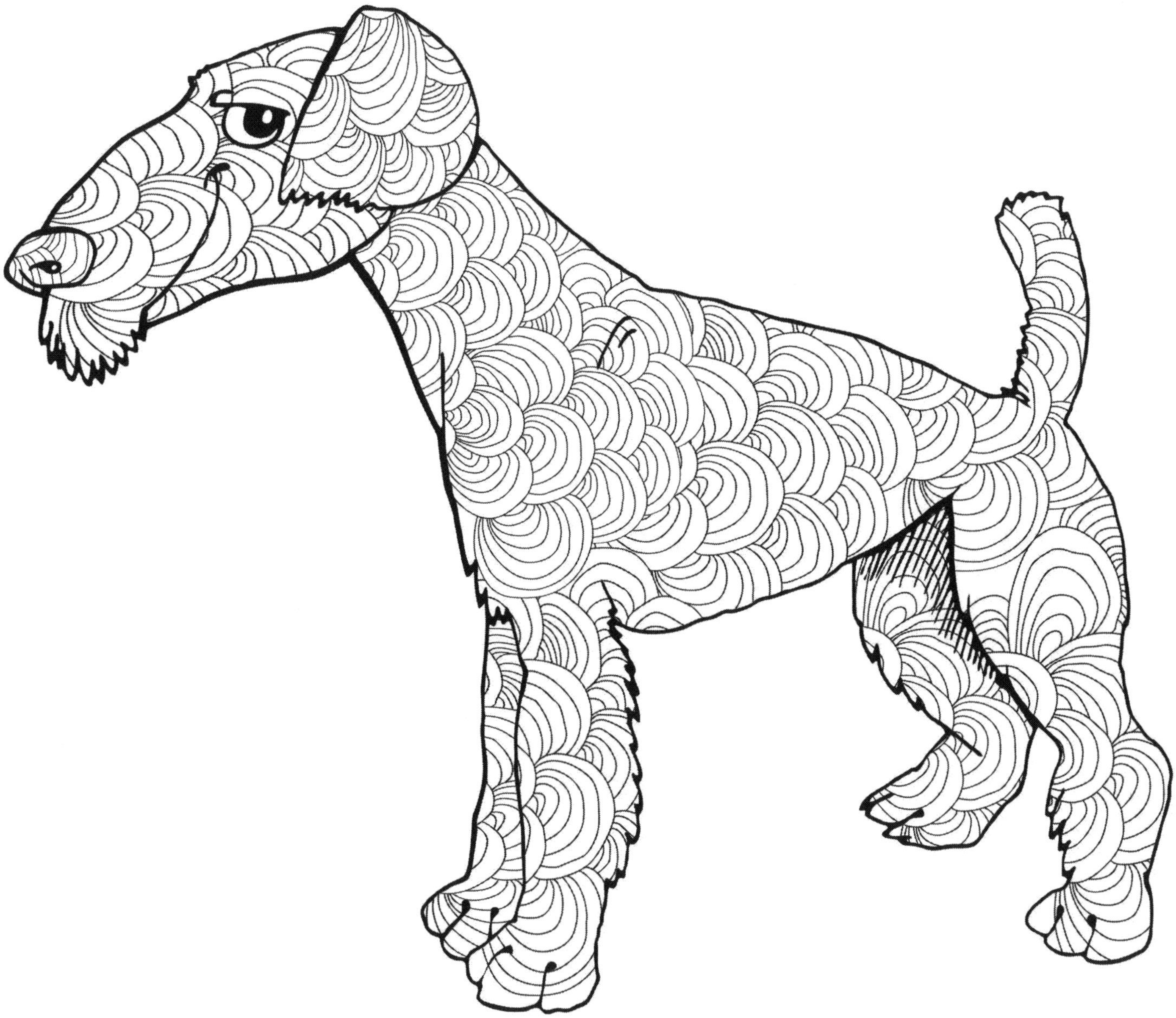

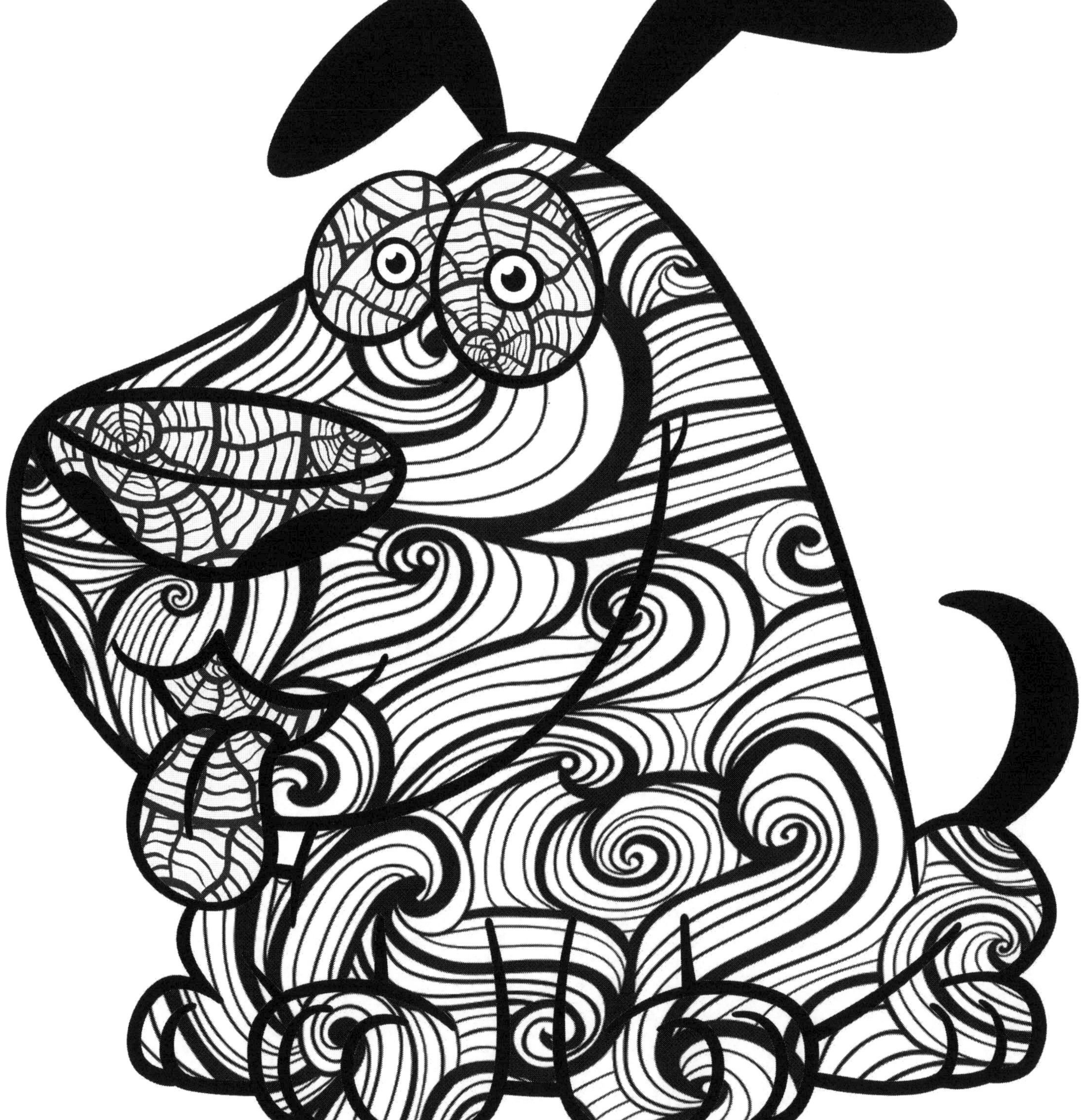

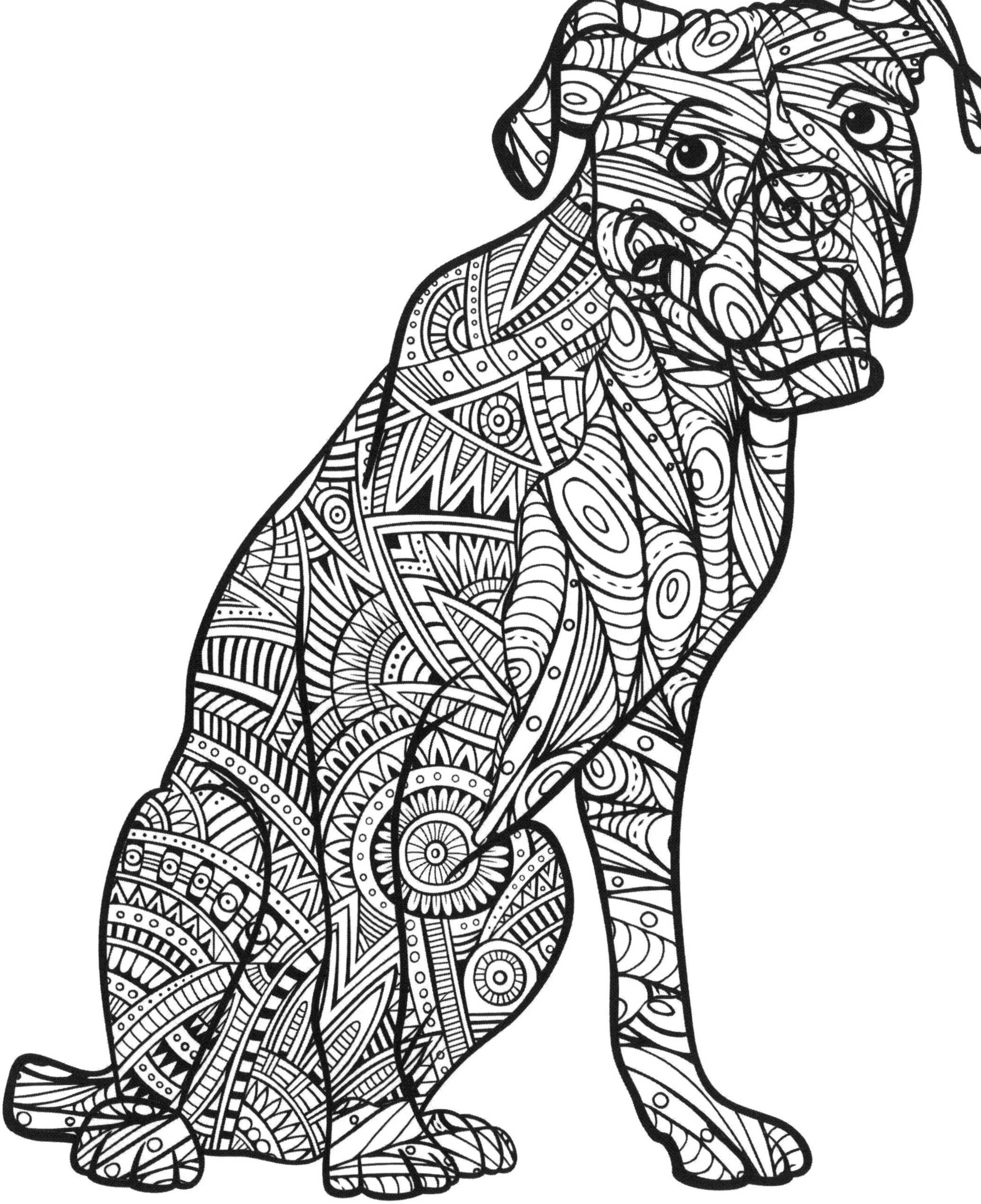

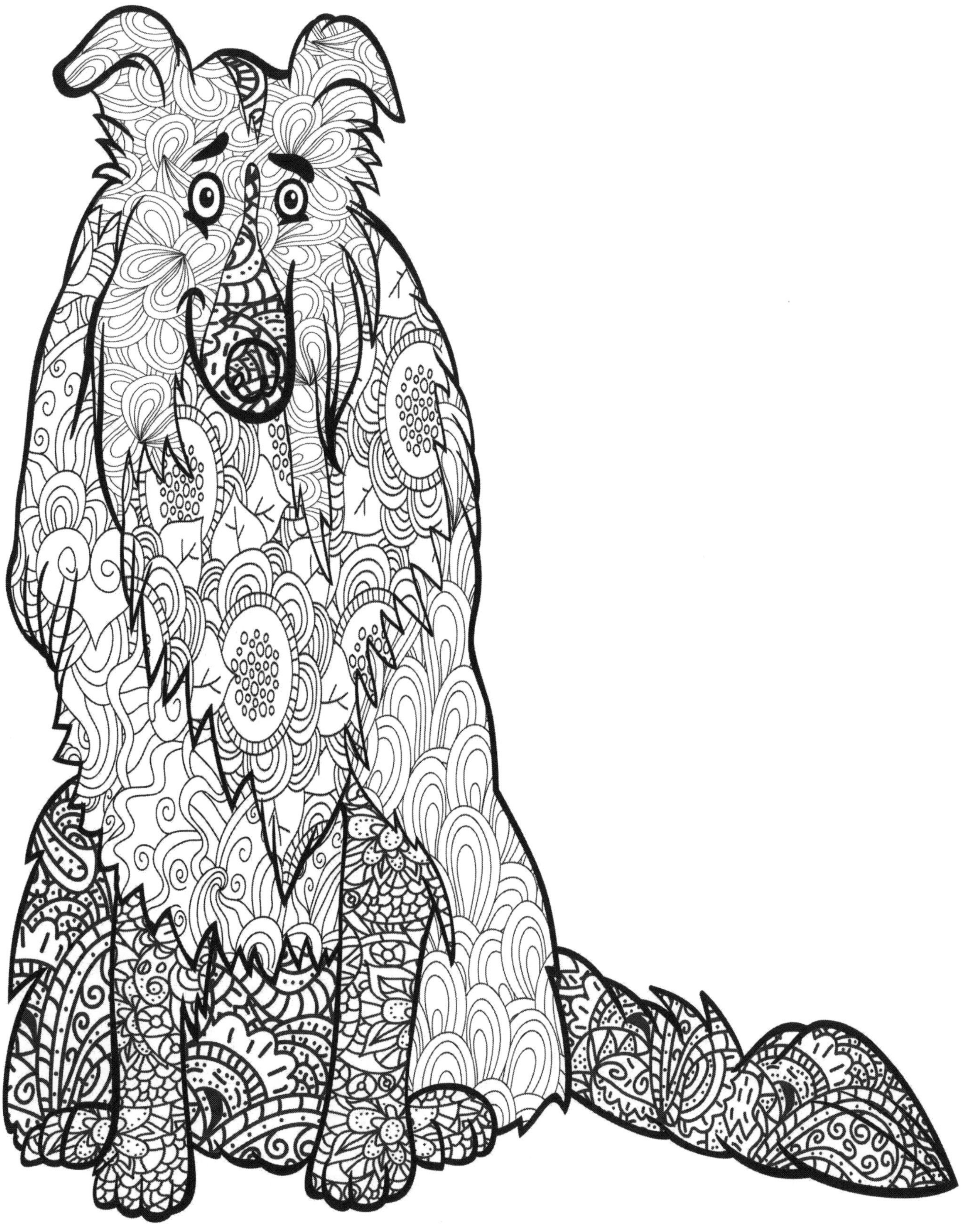